Awesome Art
Nature Art

Jeanette Ryall

WINDMILL
BOOKS
New York

Published in 2013 by Windmill Books, An Imprint of Rosen Publishing
29 East 21st Street, New York, NY10010

Copyright © 2013 by Windmill Books, An Imprint of Rosen Publishing

Produced for Windmill Books by Calcium Creative Ltd
Editor for Calcium Creative Ltd: Sarah Eason
US Editor: Sara Antill
Designer and Modelmaker: Jeanette Ryall

Photo Credits: Cover: Jeanette Ryall l, Shutterstock Thomas M Perkins r. Inside: pp. 4–5: Tudor Photography;
pp. 6–7 (main) Tudor Photography, (steps) Tudor Photography; pp. 8–9 (steps) Tudor Photography; p. 9 (main)
Tudor Photography; pp. 10–11 (steps) Tudor Photography; p. 11 (main) Tudor Photography; pp. 12–13: (steps)
Tudor Photography; p. 13: (main) Tudor Photography; p. 14 (main) Tudor Photography; pp. 14–15 (steps)
Tudor Photography; p. 15 (main) Tudor Photography; pp. 16–17: (steps) Tudor Photography; p. 17 (main) Tudor
Photography; p. 18 (steps) Tudor Photography; p. 19 (main) Tudor Photography; p. 20 (main) Jeanette Ryall;
pp. 20–21 (steps) Tudor Photography; p. 21 (main) Tudor Photography; pp. 22–23 (steps) Tudor Photography;
p. 23 (main) Tudor Photography; pp. 24–25 (steps) Tudor Photography; p. 25 (main) Tudor Photography;
pp. 26–27 (steps) Tudor Photography; p. 27 (main) Tudor Photography; pp. 28–29 (steps) Tudor Photography;
p. 29 (main) Tudor Photography.

Library of Congress Cataloging-in-Publication Data

Ryall, Jeanette.
 Nature art / by Jeanette Ryall.
    p. cm — (Awesome art)
 Includes index.
 ISBN 978-1-4488-8088-1 (library binding) — ISBN 978-1-4488-8141-3 (pbk.) —
ISBN 978-1-4488-8147-5 (6-pack)
 1. Nature craft—Juvenile literature. I. Title.
 TT160.R935 2013
 745.5—dc23

                              2012005826

Manufactured in the United States of America

CPSIA Compliance Information: Batch #B3S12WM: For Further Information contact
Windmill Books, New York, New York at 1-866-478-0556

Contents

Awesome Nature

Take a look outside. Can you see the wonderful art all around you? Nature is full of fabulous material that you can turn into art. Did you know that you can make picture frames, scarecrows, cards, and fun animal characters from nature? In this book we'll show you just how to do that.

Find out how awesome nature art can be.

You Will Need:

All the items you will need for each activity are listed on the following pages in a "You Will Need" box, like this one. Read these boxes carefully before you start to make sure that you have everything you need.

Before you start ...

• Ask your parent or caretaker for **permission** to use the equipment and space you will need for each activity.

• Find an apron to cover your clothes, or some old clothes that you don't mind getting dirty.

• Ask an adult to help you with any of the activities that require cutting.

• Wash your hands carefully after touching berries, leaves, and other outdoor items.

Feather Frame

You Will Need:

- brightly colored feathers
- scissors or art knife
- ruler • cardboard
- paint • paintbrush
- pencil • glue
- tape

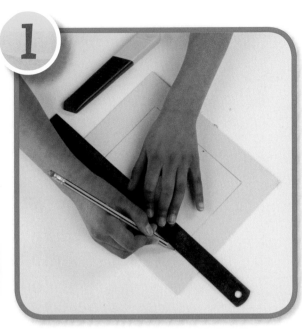

1

On a piece of cardboard, draw a rectangle 7 inches (17 cm) high by 5 inches (13 cm) wide. Use scissors to cut out the rectangle, or have an adult cut it out with an art knife.

2

Paint your picture frame with gold paint. Be sure to cover the whole frame. You may need to apply two or three **coats**, allowing each coat to dry before applying the next.

3

When the paint has dried completely, cover the frame with glue. Then stick your colored feathers to the frame. Make sure you **alternate** the colors of the feathers.

4

When you have covered the frame with feathers, leave it to dry. Then fix a favorite photograph to the back of the frame with tape.

TOP TIP
You can also use dried leaves to cover your picture frame.

CRESS MonsTeRS

You Will Need:

- eggs • spoon
- paints • paintbrush
- water • **cress seeds**
- **tissue paper**

TOP TiP
Stand your finished eggs in egg cups.

Ask an adult to boil two eggs and leave them to cool. Carefully cut the top off each egg and scoop out the inside to empty the eggshell.

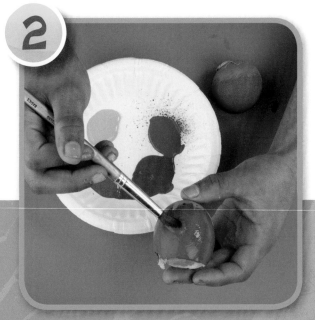

Paint each egg in a different color and put them to one side to dry. You must make sure that the paint is completely dry before painting on the face and pattern.

3

Now paint one egg with a toothy smile and the other with an angry stare! Cover both eggs with a fun, bright pattern. Leave them to dry.

4

Tear off two pieces of tissue paper and wet them with water. Place the paper inside the eggshells and sprinkle some cress seeds on top. Put the eggshells in sunlight.

After a few days your eggshells will start to turn into cress monsters!

DReam CatCHeR

You Will Need:
- **willow** twig
- thin wire • **pliers**
- thick string • thin string
- beads • feathers

1

Ask an adult to cut a piece of willow twig around 24 inches (60 cm) long. Curl it into a circle and tie it into position with some pieces of wire, as shown above.

2

Wind a long piece of thick string around the willow circle, as shown in the photograph above. Wind it thickly in five places. Tie the string into position.

3

Now wind some thin string around one of the five thick sections. Loop the string across from one section to another. Tie it into place each time, as shown in the photograph.

4

Start to form a crisscross pattern with the string. Tie the string into position as you make the pattern.

5

Thread some beads onto the end of the string and tie into position at the center of the **dream catcher**, as shown. Thread some more beads onto the end of the string.

Tie some feathers to the end of the string. Your dream catcher is complete!

Nature Picture

You Will Need:

- white construction paper
- glue • pencil • fine **gravel**
- blue paint • paintbrush • shells
- twigs • nuts • stones
- leaves • bush or **fern fronds**
- small dried orange
- knife • play sand

On a piece of paper, draw the outline of a mountain range. Paint the area above the mountains blue. This is the sky. Cover the area below with glue, then cover with sand. Shake off the **excess** sand.

Draw another shape below the mountain range for the ground. Cover it with glue and sprinkle fine gravel over the area. Leave to dry, then shake off the excess.

Glue some shells to the left side of your picture. Glue some leaves, ferns, or bush fronds to the right side of your picture. Leave the picture to dry once more.

4

Glue some small stones and a dried twig to the center of the picture. Add some nuts, more shells, and some green leaves. Leave the picture to dry again.

Cut a dried orange in half and glue it to the sky for your Sun.

TOP TIP
You can use **moss**, feathers, and flowers in your picture, too.

LOG CABIN

You Will Need:

- empty cardboard box
- scissors • tape
- glue • twigs
- tree fronds

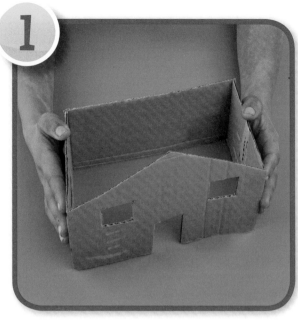

Cut your box into four same-sized sections. Cut a door and windows into one of the sections. Tape the four sides together. Cut a rectangle for the roof and fold it in the center.

Cover the roof with glue. Line the roof with your fronds, as shown. Glue one twig into position along the center of the roof.

Cover the sides of the cabin with glue. Cover all the sides with sections of cut twigs, as shown above. Make sure the twigs line up evenly as you glue them onto the cabin.

Ask an adult to cut some shorter twigs for the front of the cabin, to fit around the windows and door. Carefully glue them into position.

Finally, glue one twig to the roof to make the chimney.

TOP TiP

To add snow to your winter wonderland cabin, sprinkle flour over the roof.

CUTE SCARECROW

You Will Need:

- straw • long stick
- two short sticks • stuffing
- plastic bag • large cloth
- old clothes • two paper plates • paint
- paintbrush • wire
- glue • tape

1

To make the body of the scarecrow, tie a long stick to two shorter sticks to form a cross. Use some wire to hold the sticks in position.

2

TOP TIP

Ask a friend or an adult to hold the scarecrow while you put on the hands.

Fold two sections of straw into loops and tie them into position with straw, as shown above. Use tape to attach the straw shapes to each end of the short sticks to make the scarecrow's hands.

3

Fill a plastic bag with stuffing, then cover it with a cloth. Tie it into position on the scarecrow's body, as shown above.

4

Now you can dress your cute scarecrow with old clothes! Make sure that you ask permission to use them before you put them on the scarecrow.

Tie the pants or shorts onto your scarecrow with straw. This will stop them from falling off when you stand your scarecrow upright!

Paint the eyes, nose, cheeks, and a smiling mouth. Leave the plates to dry once more.

Paint one paper plate pink. Paint another paper plate brown. Leave them to dry. When they are dry, glue the plates together, painted side out.

Now draw the **outline** of the eyes, eyebrows, eyelashes, **nostril** shapes, and the outline of the mouth. Cut a few pieces of straw and glue them onto the paper plate face for hair.

Place the scarecrow's head onto the body and add a hat.

TOP TIP
You can make a female scarecrow by using different clothes.

stone CReatuRes

1

To make a frog, use modeling clay and glue to attach two small stones to the underside of a large, round stone, as shown above.

You Will Need:

- large and small smooth, round stones
- modeling clay
- paintbrush
- paints • glue

TOP TiP
Look at the stones you find and decide which creature they look like.

2

Roll two small pieces of your modeling clay into balls. Stick them to the top of the large, round stone, as shown in the photograph above.

3

Now paint the stone a bright green color. Make sure you cover the stone completely and don't forget to paint the two small stones.

4

When the green paint has dried, paint a spotted pattern with a darker green paint. Then paint the frog's eyes and mouth, too.

Mini YARD

You Will Need:

- tree fronds or bush cuttings • moss • empty cookie tin • dirt • fine gravel • twigs • shells • small stones • berries • small mirror • glue • animal figurines

Fill your cookie tin with dirt. You can dig up some dirt from your backyard or buy some from a store. Place a small mirror in the center of the dirt.

Add some fine gravel to the scene. Be careful not to cover the mirror. Place some small stones and shells around the outside of the gravel, as shown in the photograph above.

Press some small fronds into the dirt, as shown, to create trees for your **miniature** backyard. Add moss to the foreground. You can use grass if you don't have moss.

Complete the scene by adding some small animal figurines to the backyard. Use glue to make a cute fence from the twigs.

TOP TIP

Add some small berries to the moss to give the scene color.

Bonsai Tree

You Will Need:

- packing tape • berries
- fine wire • scissors
- small leaves
- fine gravel
- small jar

1 Ask an adult to cut 20 pieces of wire. They should be of the same length. Bunch them together and secure them into position with packing tape, as shown above.

2 Bend each piece of the wire to look like the branches of a tree. Keep the pieces grouped together in sections of three, as shown above. Shape the ends to look like twigs.

3 Continue to bend and fix the branches into the shape of a tree. Take time to make the tree now because you won't be able to bend the branches when you have put leaves and berries on them.

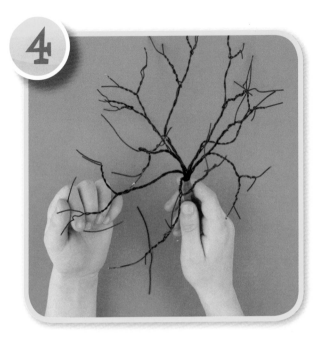

4

Trim some of the branches to make them shorter. This will make the tree look more natural. Gather lots of small leaves and berries for the next stage. Make a hole in each berry.

5

Thread the leaves and berries onto the branches of your **bonsai tree**, as shown in the photograph above. Cover the whole tree so that each branch has a leaf and a berry.

Pour some fine gravel into a small jar and set your bonsai tree in it to hold it upright.

TOP TIP

You can make lots of trees using leaves and berries of different colors.

NATURE CARDS

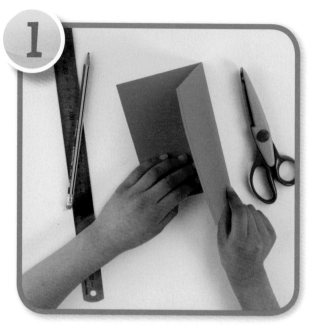

1 Draw a rectangle onto blue construction paper. Then cut it out. Fold the paper in the middle, as shown above, to make a card.

2 Tear a piece of orange construction paper, making sure that the torn edges are **ragged**. Tear off another piece of white construction paper and roll it into a **spiral** shape.

3 Glue the orange construction paper to the front of the blue card. Glue a fabric leaf onto the middle of the orange paper. Then glue on the dried flowers and the roll of white paper.

FRuity GaRLanD

You Will Need:
- strong wire • pliers
- dried cut orange sections
- small brown and cream **wicker** balls
- dried flowers
- straw • glue

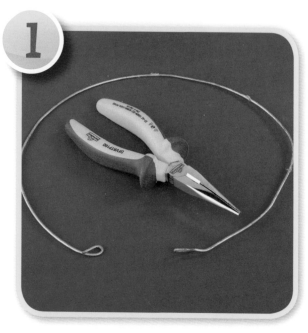

Ask an adult to cut a piece of wire for you. It should be around 24 inches (60 cm) in length. Then gently bend the wire into a circle and curl each end into a hook.

Glue three wicker balls of the same color together in a triangle shape. Repeat with all of the wicker balls.

Thread the wicker balls, dried orange sections, and dried flowers onto the wire. Continue until you have covered the wire.

4

Link the hooks at each end of the wire together. Then roll a section of straw into a bow and tie it onto the hooks, as shown above. Your **garland** is complete!

TOP TIP
You can use dried grapefruit or kiwi fruit sections, too.

GLOSSARY

alternate (OL-ter-nayt) To change every other time.

bonsai tree (bohn-SY TREE) A miniature Japanese tree.

coats (KOHTS) Coverings or layers.

cress seeds (KRES SEEDS) Seeds that grow into a cress plant.

dream catcher (DREEM KA-cher) An ornament used by Native Americans to catch bad dreams.

excess (EK-ses) Leftover material that it not needed.

fern (FERN) A type of plant with large, feathery leaves.

fronds (FRAHNDZ) The part of a branch from a tree, bush, or plant that is covered with leaves.

garland (GAR-land) A round necklace made up of flowers or other natural objects.

gravel (GRA-vel) Very small stones.

miniature (MIH-nee-uh-chur) Tiny.

moss (MOS) A plant that grows in damp places.

nostril (NOS-trul) An opening on the face or head through which air is breathed.

outline (OWT-lyn) The outer shape of something.

permission (per-MIH-shun) To be allowed to do something.

pliers (PLY-erz) Sharp tools used to cut through thick or hard material.

ragged (RA-ged) Rough and uneven.

spiral (SPY-rul) A long, coiled shape.

technique (tek-NEEK) A way of doing something.

thread (THRED) To push a length of wire, thread, or string through a hole in an object.

tissue paper (TIH-shoo PAY-per) Very thin, soft paper.

wicker (WIH-ker) Dried twigs that are wound into shapes.

willow (WIH-low) A tree with long, bendy branches.

FURTHER READING

Luxbacher, Irene. *The Jumbo Book of Outdoor Art.* Tonawanda, NY: Kids Can Press, 2006.

Martin, Laura. *Nature's Art Box.* North Adams, MA: Storey Publishing, 2003.

Monaghan, Kimberly. *Organic Crafts: 75 Earth-Friendly Activities.* Chicago: Chicago Review Press, 2007.

Websites

For web resources related to the subject of this book, go to: **www.windmillbooks.com/weblinks** and select this book's title.

InDeX